A Muslim Girl's Guide
to
Life's BIG Changes

Rayhana Khan

Ta-Ha Publishers Ltd.

Copyright © Ta-Ha Publishers Ltd. 2005 CE
First published 1426 AH/February 2005 CE
Reprinted 2006-2013, 2015, 2016, 2019, 2020, 2021

This edition published June 2014

Ta-Ha Publishers Ltd,
Unit 4, The Windsor Centre
Windsor Grove, West Norwood
London, SE27 9NT, UK
www.tahapublishers.com

Written by: Rayhana Khan
Edited by: Dr. Abia Afsar-Siddiqui
Cover Design by: Mariama Janneh
Typesetting by: Affan Aziz

A catalogue record of this book is available from the British Library.
ISBN 13: 9781842001530

Printed and Bound by: IMAK Ofset, Turkey

To My Mama...

The older I get in life the more I realise I need you. May Allah protect you always.

(Ameen)

"Fear Allah wherever you may be; follow up an evil deed with a good one which will wipe (the former) out, and behave good-naturedly towards people."

(at-Tirmidhi)

Contents

Introduction

To my younger sister, As salaamu alaikum.

Congratulations! You are no longer considered a little girl but rather a growing adult!

I am sure that you no longer 'play' anymore and are now wanting to spend more and more time with your friends, wanting to go shopping with them for the latest 'must-haves' and having fun with them. After all, this is an exciting time in your life.

Sometimes, however, you may find that life at school with your friends can be very different to your life at home and this can lead to some confusion about what to do. This does not mean that growing up has to be boring for you. What it does mean is that as a young Muslim lady growing up in a non-Muslim environment, there are many things that you need to be aware of in order to become a fine Muslim woman, insha Allah, and this is where the challenge lies for you.

I hope that this book will help you in the years ahead by tackling some of the important issues that may affect you.

Take care and always remember my advice to you as an older sister who has been through what you are about to experience: 'Stop, think and question all that you do in your life.'

May Allah guide you through the coming years and make them easy for you. Ameen.

Wasalaam,

Rayhana Khan

Friends and School Life

 School life is often fun as well as challenging. You will build a network of friends from all backgrounds, cultures, religions and meet many people with differing opinions from your own.

Your hours spent at school are often testing ones as you are surrounded not only by your peers but also those who are older than you.

As you go further and further into your school life you may start to feel that the people you hang out with are your new found 'family' since you spend most of your waking day with them.

As time passes and your friendship group grows, you want to start looking like them, talking like them and even walking like them, so that you can fit into the group. You may begin to dress as your friends do, enjoy the same things as them and hang out in the same places as they do.

'So what's wrong with wanting to be like my friends?' you ask.

Well, this depends on who your friends are. If your friends are out just to have fun - fun at parties with alcohol and music and boys - if your friends do not dress Islamically, perform their salah, respect their elders, then you must ask yourself if your friends are good for you. How far would you go to please them?

It is vital to choose the correct friendship group, as friends can either make or break you. The Prophet ﷺ has said:

'You shall be raised on the Day of Judgement with those you spent your life with.' (Sahih Bukhari)

As time passes you will notice that your friends' views and ideas are having an impact on you. They begin to influence the way you look, speak and behave. It is guaranteed that your friends will leave a lifetime impression on you, so be mindful of whom you choose to befriend.

The qualities you should be looking for in a true friend are honesty, someone who knows right from wrong and those who can overcome the pressures of looking and sounding like everyone else.

Time should be spent with girls who understand the importance of behaving correctly, those who know that every action impacts on their overall character. Your peers have the unique quality of being able to mould you into something other than what perhaps is being taught at home. This may result in you leading two lives - one which is in line with your family's ideas and another which makes you popular amongst your group of friends. If you are true to yourself you will know whether you are losing your true identity or not.

Part of growing up is about having your independence and freedom to be able to mix with your friends outside of school time. There is no harm in this so long as you abide by some simple rules. You must always seek permission from your parents before going out and also inform them of who you will be with and what you will be doing. You must ensure that you return home at the time they tell you to; breaking your parents trust should not be taken lightly.

Everyone experiences pressure now and again when in the company of others and you may often find yourself torn between your friends and your religion. Having the strength to fight peer pressure can be a difficult thing. We are not perfect but we have been given the intelligence to know right from wrong, we are all capable of fighting temptation and standing up for what we believe in. Remember, Shaytan awaits us at every stage of our day, waiting to pounce on us from the moment we awake to the time we retire to bed. Shaytan presents himself in many types and forms through music, literature, TV and you've guessed it…through our friends.

How to fight peer pressure…

● Shield yourself from such pressures by surrounding yourself with good role models as friends. Remember a small group of friends are far better than a whole gang of friends who will lead you astray;

● Be proud of who you are. Don't feel intimidated by those who you know are in the wrong;

● Question your actions as well as your friends in hope of achieving the right decision;

● Seek guidance and support from your family, older friends, etc. who have all experienced what you are facing;

● Always turn to Allah who will steer you in the right direction.

> **'A person is likely to follow the faith of his friend, so look to whom you befriend.' (Abu Dawud)**

What do we Believe in?

What is Islam all about?

It is a complete way of life. You see, Allah has created human beings and He knows us best. He has given us His book, the Qur'an, which tells us what is right and wrong. He also sent down the Beloved Prophet Muhammad ﷺ and we have his example or Sunnah to guide us in the form of the Hadith.

Allah has told us the rules and regulations that we must stick by so that we can be happy both as individuals and also as a society. Sometimes it might seem like there are a lot of rules and we might not understand why we have to do something. But we trust that, because Allah made us, He knows best.

> **'The Quran will either be evidence for you or against you.' (Sahih Muslim)**

Allah has explained that the life of this world (Dunya) is temporary, but there is a life after death (Akhirah), which is forever. Our actions in this life will determine what our eternal life will be like in the Akhirah. We can either be rewarded with Paradise or punished in Hell.

So you must be very careful about how you spend your time in this world and the consequences of your actions, both for yourself and for others, because Allah is always watching. If you follow Allah's commands, then He will be pleased with you. However hard it may seem, Allah's pleasure is more important than the pleasure of anyone else. So whenever you do something, the first thing you must ask yourself is whether it will please Allah.

I know that this may not always be easy. When you look around you, no matter where you are - on the streets, on TV, on advertisement hoardings - you will see that the world has become a place where there is very little modesty (haya) and consideration for others, two qualities which are very important in Islam. People are only interested in themselves and doing what pleases them without thinking about others. You can see these things through people's behaviour, language, actions and through what they are wearing (or not, as the case may be).

You may ask yourself, 'Who is to blame?' Is it us, society or is it the media? The answer is a combination of these things but as Muslims, we should avoid the temptations that we face all around us - temptations that have been put in our way by Shaytan, who wants us to go astray.

Unfortunately, many of us have more than befriended Shaytan and forgotten what Prophet Muhammad ﷺ did for us. He spent his life establishing rights for all human beings, spreading the word of Allah, being mocked and even tortured for doing this just so that we could have the privilege of practising Islam. He worried about us and shed tears for us. So how can we show our love for this great and noble man? By continuing to live according to the Qur'an and Sunnah and by avoiding the temptations around us.

Two of the most important things that we should do on a regular basis are prayer (salah) and fasting (sawm).

As a Muslim, you are required to pray or perform salah five times a day. Salah is an opportunity for you to take some 'time out' from whatever you are doing and remember Allah and His blessings upon you. It is your chance to get closer to Allah and away from the stresses of this world. The Prophet ﷺ said that,

> 'The key to Paradise is Salah and the key to Salah
> is cleanliness.'
> (Hadith from at-Tirmidhi)

You will need to perform at least one salah while you are at school, which is probably the Dhuhr or midday salah. Most schools have a small room that you can offer salah in, or if not, they will be able to provide you a space if you ask politely.

There is no excuse for not offering your salah (except if you are menstruating - see chapter 7). It may be easy to forget when you are catching up on the latest gossip at lunchtime with your friends. This is another reason for keeping good company so that your friends can remind you to perform salah if you forget or better still, you can all pray together.

You must perform salah even if you are on a school trip, although you can shorten it while you are travelling. It is very important that you perform salah regularly as the Prophet ﷺ said,

'What lies between a person and disbelief is the abandonment of prayer.'
(Hadith from Sahih Muslim, Abu Dawud and an-Nasa'i)

Once a year, the month of fasting or Ramadan comes around. This month is a blessing from Allah to Muslims and in this month we put aside some of the pleasures of this world and take some time out to think about the things that Allah has given us and how lucky we are. By not eating or drinking during the day, we can understand what it feels like to be hungry. This makes us appreciate those that are hungry every day through no choice of their own and it makes us grateful for our blessings from Allah.

As well as not eating and drinking during daylight hours, we must also be even more careful than usual about not lying, arguing or back-biting.

Again, it is very important that you are careful about observing sawm (except if you are menstruating - see chapter 7) and taking advantage of all the blessings that this month has to offer. The Prophet ﷺ said that,

> 'Whoever fasts Ramadan with faith and expectation of reward, his previous sins are forgiven.'
> (Sahih Bukhari)

You should also try to avoid going out unnecessarily in this month no matter how tempting it may seem, and use this month to reflect more about Islam and learn something that perhaps you didn't know about before.

If you take care of your salah and your fasts then Allah will take care of you, insha Allah, and what better friend and helper than Allah?

> 'The fasting person has at the time of breaking his fast a du'a that is not rejected.' (Ibn Majah)

How You Can Become Closer To Allah

There are many ways in which you can spend your time constructively and become closer to Allah.

● **Reading the QUR'AN**

The Qur'an is the Word of Allah which was revealed to our Beloved Prophet Muhammad ﷺ through the Angel Jibra'il. There are two reasons why you should read it regularly.

Simply reading the Qur'an in Arabic with your full attention is in itself an act of worship and will bring you closer to Allah.

The Qur'an is a guide given to us by Allah and so it contains plenty of useful and relevant advice about how best to live our lives. So, by reading it, understanding what it says and acting upon it you will become closer to Allah and insha Allah a better Muslim.

Even reading a few lines regularly every day, you will find that you can finish the whole Qur'an at least twice in a year.

It is also important to memorise small verses from the Qur'an so that you can recite them in your salah. The Holy Prophet ﷺ said,

> "The person who has nothing of the Qur'an inside him is like an empty or ruined house."
> (at-Tirmidhi)

- **DU'A**

Du'a, which means 'calling upon', is a very personal way of communicating with Allah. You can choose what you say and which language you say it in, but there are some recommended ways in which to make du'a.

The Prophet ﷺ used to make du'a by facing the Qibla and raising his cupped hands towards the sky. When you make du'a, it is good to thank Allah for all that He has given you and to send salat and salam to the Holy Prophet ﷺ and his family. You can ask for anything as long as it is halal and does not involve asking Allah to harm or hurt anyone else. You can ask for forgiveness, strength, guidance, good health, good exam results, good things in this world and in the Akhirah. Be sure to pray for your loved ones, including those who have passed away. You can pray for those that are less fortunate than you and especially those who are suffering as a result of war, natural disasters etc.

You must not lose hope if your du'a is not answered immediately. If that was the case it would mean Allah would become our servant waiting for our requests instead of our Master. For your du'a to be answered you have to work towards becoming closer to Allah. Remember Allah is the best of planners. Your prayers will, insha Allah, be accepted when the time is right but you have to be patient.

● DHIKR

Another way of becoming closer to Allah is through dhikr (the remembrance of Allah).

> Allah has mentioned in the Quran that:
> 'Remember Me and I shall remember you.'
> (2:152)

You can do dhikr at any time of the day, while you are walking, sitting or even when you can't sleep. You can spend as little as a few seconds reciting a few words either in your mind, on your fingers or on a tasbih. The following words carry a great reward:

> SubhanAllah - Glory be to Allah
> Alhamdulillah - All praise and thanks is due to Allah
> La ilaha illallah - There is no god but Allah
> Allahu Akbar - Allah is the Greatest
> Astaghfirullah - I seek Allah's forgiveness

• By performing a SUNNAH

The word sunnah means 'practice'. When you carry out a sunnah you are copying the actions and sayings of the Prophet Muhammad ﷺ who is the best example of how we should behave. By following the noble practices of our Prophet ﷺ we are in fact becoming better Muslims. It does not have to be difficult or time consuming to perform a sunnah. For example, the Prophet ﷺ would always begin his meal with the words 'Bismillahir rahmanir raheem' and eat with his hands. He would always finish his food and he never criticised the taste of food.

It is little actions such as these which will help others to warm to Islam and earn you a great reward from Allah.

• SADAQAH

Sadaqah is when you do something generous for others only for the pleasure of Allah. It may be as simple as smiling at someone to cheer them up, picking up litter from the street or perhaps not buying some sweets for yourself one day and giving the money to charity. When you do something selfless for someone else then Allah is very pleased and He rewards you both in this world and in the Hereafter.

> The Prophet ﷺ said, "...Sadaqah destroys
> sins as water extinguishes fire..." (Mishkat)

What are you Wearing?

 If you look at any of the magazines for teenagers or for women, then you will see glossy pictures and read articles about the latest beauty products, trendiest styles of clothing, must-have fashion accessories and latest hairstyles of the season.

Are these really the concerns of a young Muslimah? Unfortunately, in reality, the answer is Yes.

Why do we feel that before we can leave the front door to go anywhere, we must spend hours doing our hair, squeeze into whatever little item of clothing happens to be in fashion, plaster our faces with foundation, blusher, lipstick (the list goes on...), and finish off with a generous spray of perfume? And that if we don't do all of this, we are not presentable?

> 'Allah does not look at your outward appearance but only your hearts and deeds.' (Sahih Muslim)

Perhaps you think that it is uncool, unflattering and old-fashioned to wear loose and covering clothing. Anyway, what could be the harm in dressing in the latest fashions and wearing make-up, you may think. After all, everyone else is doing it.

You might ask whether the way you dress is all that important - after all, you perform your salah regularly and fast every Ramadan. I don't wish to scare you but this is what the Prophet ﷺ had to say about women who dress inappropriately, 'If you see them (women dressed inappropriately) curse them because they will be deprived of the mercy of Allah.' (Part of a Hadith from Musnad Ahmed)

So, let's start by looking at what the Qur'an and the Hadith say about how a Muslimah should dress.

This depends on who you are with. If you are with Muslim ladies, very young children and mahram men (mahrams are men that you can never get married to and these are your grandfather, father, father's brother, mother's brother, your brother and nephew), then you can wear perfume, make-up, jewellery and trendy clothes. You do not have to cover your hair in front of these people, but your clothes should remain within the bounds of decency.

If there are non-mahrams present (that includes your male cousins), even in your own home, or you are going out then you must cover your whole body except for your face and hands in loose-fitting clothes that should not be see through. You should not wear make-up or perfume and if you are wearing jewellery then this should not be showing or making any noise. These are the basic requirements of Hijab according to Surat an-Nur ayat 30-31 and various ahadith.

This means that dressing in clothes which are short, tight or revealing is haram. To go out into the streets without your hair covered is haram. To wear make-up while there are non-mahram boys/men around is haram. To wear perfume while outside or in the company of non-mahram men is haram. To wear jewellery which jingles even though it can't be seen is haram. To imitate the clothes and hairstyle of men is haram. To get changed in front of anyone is haram.

So why are the rules for Islamic dress so detailed? You see, by dressing in a particular way, you give an impression of yourself to other people: fellow Muslims, non-Muslims and boys. Ask yourself what impression you would like other people to have of you?

By correcting your external appearance and dressing Islamically:

● You are identifying yourself as a Muslim to your fellow Muslims.

● You are showing non-Muslims that you are proud to be a Muslim.

● You are showing people that you are an intelligent and independent young lady who is not pressured into 'looking like everyone else' and that you want to be respected for your personality and your brains rather than your body.

● You are effectively telling members of the opposite sex that you are a respectable girl not one that tries to attract male attention.

● Most importantly, Allah will be pleased with you.

I never said it would be easy, especially if your family do not dress Islamically. In fact, why not be a role model to your friends and family, Muslims and non-Muslims alike, who will respect you and perhaps be inspired by your strength, character and ability to be your own, independent, free-thinking person?

As Muslims, we should not be embarrassed to dress Islamically. If anything, it is those people that expose their bodies to the world in tight and revealing clothes that should be ashamed and embarrassed.

So next time you open your wardrobe, think about how you wish to be seen by the world.

How are you Behaving?

 We have just looked at how appearances send out impressions about you. But equally important are your language and behaviour. There is no point dressing Islamically if you don't behave Islamically.

So what does Islam say about how to behave with different people?

Friends

You know the importance of having friends that will not distract you from your religion or ask you to do things that are against Islam, regardless of their race or their religion. But you must be friendly and kind to everyone. It is important to have good Muslim friends as well, whether this is in school or outside.

Parents

Parents are given the highest respect in Islam. You must never ever be rude to them, shout at them or answer back to them. You might see your friends or youngsters on TV being rude to their parents but this is very wrong. Your parents have done so much for you that you should not hurt their feelings. Your parents love you very much and are always concerned about what is right for you. You should always try to please them, provided of course that what they ask you to do does not go against Islam. The Prophet ﷺ said that when an obedient child looks with love at his parents he gets the reward equal to that of going on pilgrimage. Can you really afford not to carry out your duty towards the two most important people in your life?

Teachers

Teachers are like your parents in school. Islam tells us to always respect them. Avoid playing the class joker just to impress you friends. Teachers are valuable people, building a good relationship with them means you can turn to them for help, support and guidance regarding matters both in and outside of school.

Boys

You will notice that the girls in your class are starting to take an interest in boys now. They are starting to wear tight and revealing clothes to attract the attention of boys. All of this is strictly haram. Islam is very clear that a Muslim girl should have no relationship with a non-mahram boy of any kind. In fact, you should not even mix with boys at all. It is easy to see why.

Some girls spend a long time sending out signals, trying to make themselves look attractive for boys and trying to catch their attention. Then once they have his attention, they get into tricky situations and are left feeling emotional and upset at the very least, if not hurt and in serious trouble. They do this because they think that they need the attention of boys to feel good. They think that it is alright to use their body to have fun with boys. As a beautiful Muslimah, you do not need a boy to tell you that you look nice and remember your body is far too precious to be used for fun and games. Your body is Allah's gift to you, you must look after it.

General

You must always be very polite and respectful to anyone that is older than you, regardless of their race or religion. You must be very kind to those who are younger than you. You should try not to be angry with anyone or argue with anyone, after all, Islam is a kind and gentle religion. It is important that you do not use bad language at any time, that you do not say anything bad about anyone and that you are always honest. As well as showing love and respect to our fellow human beings, Islam also teaches us to treat animals and the environment with the same respect. It is our duty to treat all animals (including insects that don't harm) with love and ensure that no harm comes to them while they are in our care. Because Allah has created the world and all that is in it, we must not abuse our surroundings by creating unnecessary pollution and we must try not to be wasteful of resources such as water and paper.

Insha Allah by taking care of your actions, language and behaviour, you will be respected by everyone.

> "The most beloved of Allah's servants to Allah are those with the best manners."
> (Sahih Bukhari)

Heroines

Throughout our life many people will come and go, and in some way big or small, each one of them will have an impact on our character, thoughts and actions.

We may find strength and courage in people we know as well as being inspired by those we see on TV or read about in magazines: athletes, singers, models, and actors etc. As glamorous and successful as their lives may seem to us, their gains and successes are momentary; today they are held in high esteem, tomorrow they may be forgotten by those who claim to be their 'fans'.

True success isn't about money, dress size or material things. True success is standing firm in your beliefs, regardless of the circumstances; striving to do the right thing, even when it is a struggle. It is this type of success that leads to bliss in the Hereafter.

In Islam, there are many great women we can look up to, take strength from, be inspired by and be reminded of our real goals in life. Sayyidah Asiyah ﷺ was the Queen of Egypt; she had everything that her heart desired: fine dining, beautiful clothes, a huge palace, stunning jewellery and maids were just a few of the bounties that she possessed. Yet, despite all this, her heart did not find peace in these things or the harsh rulings of her husband – Pharaoh. Having met and cared for Musa ﷺ, Asiyah's ﷺ heart softened towards his message of believing in One God. She kept her beliefs secret from her husband who would order his army to torture those who believed in the Oneness of God. Finally, her secret was known to the Pharaoh, who did his best to persuade her to believe otherwise. However, Asiyah's ﷺ love for Allah ﷻ grew stronger and she gave up her status as Queen; she ran away to seek guidance from Allah but was soon arrested, tortured and burned. The Pharaoh ordered his men to nail her to the ground and put a heavy boulder on her chest under the scorching sun, yet before her death, she made a du'a to Allah ﷻ by saying,

"My Lord! Build for me a home with You in Jannah and save me from Pharaoh and his works." (66:11)

Asiyah ﷺ was a remarkable lady who gave up her fame, fortune, freedom and endless luxuries for the sake of Allah ﷻ and as result has been described in the Quran by Allah ﷻ as,

"An example for those who believe." (66: 11-12)

She was without a doubt, a true role model for us all to follow.

Another great lady of the past was described by the angels in Surah Al-Imran as the one whom Allah 'has chosen, made pure and exalted above all women in the world'; it is none other than Maryum ﷺ, the mother of Isa ﷺ. No other woman has been given more attention in the Quran. Maryum ﷺ has been mentioned 34 times, with an entire chapter named after her.

Maryum ﷺ placed her complete trust in Allah ﷻ during a time that her family and community shunned her and accused her of being unchaste. However, she remained patient to Allah's Will; her sincerity, strength, piety and purity to Allah are qualities that all Muslims aspire to and act as a reminder to us not to give up hope or be dragged down by gossip and lies, when in fact we know the truth about our given situation.

Other great women of the past include the Prophet's ﷺ beloved wives and daughters, who gave up the luxuries of this world to live a life of simplicity and dignity.

Not all role models can be found in history books or are famous. Our next outstanding role model is one who works round the clock. Regardless of her qualifications, she manages to be a great teacher, Michelin-star chef, accountant, referee, peacemaker, diplomat, has mastered the art of playing doctors & nurses, runs a successful laundrette, taxi-service, a lost and found service as well as being the one who happily neglects her own needs in the hurry to protect, comfort, love, nurture, console and be your pillar of support. I am in fact referring to your mother; an incredible lady who often is the unsung heroine.

No one other than a mother will have the natural ability to stop and drop for their child, be it day or night, whether she is well or sick, happy or grumpy! What motivates her is not money but rather knowing you are safe, healthy and happy. Take some time to stop and realise what a gem of a person you live with. Learn to appreciate your mum; don't just take hot meals, clean clothes and money from her, but instead take from her the lessons of patience, selflessness, humility, determination and strength that she shows you each and every day.

> Bahz ibn Hakim's grandfather said, "I asked, 'Messenger of Allah, to whom should I be dutiful?'
> 'Your mother,' he replied. I asked, 'Then whom?'
> 'Your mother,' he replied. I asked, 'Then whom?'
> 'Your mother,' he replied. I asked, 'Then to whom should I be dutiful?' 'Your father,' he replied, 'and then the next closest relative and then the next."
> (Sahih Bukhari)

How are you Spending your Time?

Your friends may now be spending time at parties or even going to clubs. These places have boys and girls mixing freely with each other. People may also be drinking alcohol and smoking.

It is very important that you do not go to these places with your friends. This is strictly haram.

I remember that when I was in secondary school (not so long ago!) the school council organised a massive ball. A tent was hired for the occasion, a DJ was invited to play and, being an all girls school, we were allowed to invite a boy to the school as our dance partner.

As tickets were being sold for the big night, many of my friends tried to persuade me to attend by telling me that I would be missing out on the biggest event in the social calendar and what harm would it do if I went.

Unfortunately, not only did my non-Muslim classmates attend so too did many of the Muslim girls. Alhamdulillah, Allah gave me the courage and strength to say 'no'. You may by all means, go out with your good friends with your parents' permission. You may decide to go to a halal restaurant for lunch or go to each other's houses. But always know what is halal fun and what is haram fun and be prepared to stand up and say no to anything haram. Always be mindful of your salah at the correct times. Islam does not say that you shouldn't have fun, but you should enjoy yourself in a good way that does not hurt you or other people.

Islam values education and knowledge very much for both girls and boys therefore it is important that you work hard and do your best at school. You must not get side tracked by fashion and boys and parties. These are haram and they will also not help you in your studies.

Another thing you need to be careful about is listening to music. Unfortunately, most pop / R&B / rap music these days contains bad language, explicit lyrics and deals with matters that are not appropriate for Muslims. It is also haram to listen to these. Try your best not to overload your mp3 players, iPhones and computers with such music; instead there are a number of beautiful nasheeds available now that are relaxing, thought provoking and are a better choice of 'music'.

> **'Shaytan runs through the human body like blood runs through the veins.' (Sahih Bukhari)**

Also be careful about what you watch on TV as this influences the way you think. You should not be watching anything that contains explicit scenes, violence or bad language. Having said that, there are also a number of halal and informative programmes that you can watch in moderation.

You should also be mindful about how you use the internet. The net is an excellent source of information, however, care must be taken about which sites you log onto and more importantly what information you give out. You must stay clear of adult sites and never should you give out personal details over the net no matter how safe it seems.

Remember you are in this world to please Allah, therefore minimise the things which will steer you away from being close to Allah. If your parents do not feel it necessary for you to own a mobile phone, respect their wishes. Be true to yourself, do you want a mobile simply to keep up with everyone else or do you really need one? Don't allow your phone to be used as a tool for deception.

As with everything, it is important to strike a balance.

Double Act

Many of the Muslim youth of today are leading a double life. With so much conflicting pressure from various quarters to look or behave in a particular way, it can sometimes be much easier to just give in to the pressure and be like the people you happen to be with at the time. This is the 'chameleon' Muslimah. At home she is the modestly dressed, soft-spoken and quiet daughter, who performs her salah when her parents ask her to.

But outside the home, when she is with her friends, she wants to feel like she belongs with them. So she dresses in more fashionable clothes that may be more revealing, she might be a little louder and less modest in her speech and not so careful about her prayers. Sometimes, it can go further and the 'chameleon' Muslimah hides the truth from her parents about where she is, who she is with and what she is doing.

But you don't always need to be out of the house or wearing different clothes to lead two lives. So many young Muslimahs dress and behave according to the Qur'an and Sunnah, are proud of their identity and present a consistent face to everyone they meet. Then it all changes when she logs on to the internet and she morphs into 'cyber' Muslimah.

'Cyber' Muslimah begins her transformation by ditching her birth name, often chosen by her parents with great care, and instead replaces this with something far more upbeat, catchy and meaningful. This is accompanied by a close-up picture of herself with make-up and latest hair-do. Finally, this formerly well-spoken Muslimah adopts new language, style and attitude that are much more street cred.

In the comfort of her own room, whilst under the roof of her parents, 'cyber' Muslimah is now ready and geared up to step into the big wide world of social networking. Here she has the opportunity to be who she wants, with whom she wants and whenever she wants. All this without leaving her front door or explaining her actions to Mum and Dad!

So where might 'cyber' Muslimah hang out? Well, of course, there's Facebook which is 'cyber' Muslimah's place of choice to pick up new friends, reconnect with old ones and nose into other people's lives. Then after that she can have four different conversations on MSN at any one time. If FB or MSN seem like yesterday's entertainment then there's always Bebo, Hi5, e-buddy or even random chat rooms and forums for 'cyber'

Muslimah to explore. All this time, 'cyber' Muslimah's parents are happy because they think she is glued to the computer screen slaving over her latest assignment.

At this point, those of you reading will either realise that you are 'chameleon' or 'cyber' Muslimah or you will know some-one who is. So what's the issue?

Well the problem is that leading a double life, whether it is in real life or in cyberspace, is being a hypocrite. Ask yourself: would you be happy for your parents to see your 'cyber' perso-na or to bump into you when you are out with your friends or would you be ashamed? If you would minimise a window on your PC when your parents came into the room or cross the road to avoid them, then that means you are cheating yourself and the people around you.

Is it right to take advantage of the fact that Mum and Dad trust you to get on with your schoolwork or be at a friend's house when you might actually be on FB or out and about? You may be able to hide your double life from your parents or the com-munity but Allah is Al-Baseer, the All Seeing, you will never be able to hide from the One who is All Knowing.

My sincere advice to you is to think very carefully about who you take as a friend, because on the Day of Judgement you will be raised with the people whose company were in. Do you want to be friends with people who lead double lives, are hypocrites and do not respect their religion? If they can lie to their parents who love them and look after them, what kind of friends will they be to you? This is true for the real world as well the cyber world. Be careful of whom you spend time with online or whom you invite or accept as 'friends' to join or view your page. If it is haram to have a relationship of any kind with a non-mahram male in the real world, then the same thing is true online.

Ideally there is no need to be on every social networking site there is. However, if you feel that you really need to have an online presence, then please be cautious about what you relay and show about yourself. Be sure to implement privacy settings by restricting viewing access, only accepting and giving invitations to those you know or those you can truly benefit from. I'm not asking you to close down every account but limit such activities, keep it in perspective and don't allow your device to rule over what's really important in life.

Be true to yourself in all situations, be it when face to face with others, through your words spoken down the phone, through the texts sent to others or even when sat in front of your web cam. Be mindful that every action is being recorded by the angels and your limbs will speak either for you or against you on the Day of Judgement.

A note to those of you who know a 'chameleon' or 'cyber' Muslimah: Alhamdulillah you are true to yourself and realise the value of upholding the 'real' you to everyone around you. But that doesn't mean that you can sit back and be smug! You have a duty to let your friends know if they are going down a path that will earn them the displeasure of Allah or will compromise their dignity and safety.

A note to any parents reading: Please be aware of all the latest activities that children of your age group may be involved in, online or otherwise. Do not allow your children to pull the wool over your eyes; show them that you are on top of things…show them that you are part of THEIR world.

> 'Part of someones being a good Muslim is his leaving alone that which does not concern him.'
> (at-Tirmidhi)

What's Happening to your Body?

You will find that your body is changing now that you are a young lady. This phase is called puberty and happens between the age of 9 and 15 and lasts for 2-4 years.

So what are these changes?

You will notice thicker and darker hair growth under your arms (underarm hair) and private parts (pubic hair).

Your breasts will start to enlarge and your body shape will start to change to become more curvy. It is important that you wear clothes that do not emphasise your curves, but cover them loosely.

The biggest change...

You will start to menstruate or have 'periods' every month. For about 7 days each month, you will experience blood flow from your private part. For the first couple of days you may feel tired or irritable, you may have cramps in your stomach or sore breasts. This is perfectly normal and a natural part of growing up.

It is important to remember that a period is not an illness, nor should it be looked upon as something un-natural or dirty. It is a natural process and a part of growing up and is considered a blessing from Allah.

For the duration of your blood flow, you cannot perform salah, you cannot fast, you cannot touch the Qur'an or perform tawaaf. However, you can recite darud, make dhikr and du'a. You should not stop remembering Allah just because you cannot pray. You do not have to make up the missed salah but you should make up any missed fasts at a later date before the next Ramadan.

You must wash any clothing that has blood stains on it to purify it just as you would purify clothing with any other stain on it.

So why is this happening?

All of these changes are a blessing from Allah and mark your transition from childhood into adulthood. These changes physically prepare your body to have a baby when you get married, insha Allah.

Taking Care of your Body

Your body is Allah's gift to you and so you should look after it as best you can because you will return to Allah one day. For example, if you borrow a book from the library, the librarian will expect that you return the book in its original condition, without scribbling in it or bending the pages. In the same way, Allah expects that we will return our body to Him in the best possible condition.

Personal hygiene is extremely important in Islam as Allah has said in the Qur'an that He loves the pure ones (9:108). You should try to keep your body as clean as possible by bathing/showering regularly (it is Sunnah to bathe on a Friday before Dhuhr salah) and by doing wudu before salah five times a day.

Wudu refreshes you and cleans parts of the body that you may not normally think about such the nostrils and behind the ears.

Did you know that if you make wudu regularly, those parts of your body will shine on the Day of Judgement?
(Hadith from Sahih Muslim)

It is important that you keep your nails short. Many girls like to keep their nails long but this means that dirt can collect behind the long nails and this is unhygienic especially when you eat. You should also not paint your nails with nail polish as this will invalidate your wudu.

You should remove the hair under your arms and on your private parts regularly but certainly no less frequently than once every 40 days. This stops the bacteria from spreading and the sweat from smelling. You may remove the hair from your legs and arms if you feel it is necessary. However, you must not shape your eyebrows as this is haram. You should keep your head hair clean and combed and avoid dying it with anything other than henna (mehndi).

It is important to pay special attention to the mouth as bacteria builds faster here than anywhere else in the body. A miswak (soft stick used as a toothbrush) is an excellent way of keeping the mouth clean and smelling fresh as well as being the cure for over 70 illnesses, such as headache and gum disease.

You are not allowed to make any marks on your body such as tattoos, even the temporary ones. This includes stick-on dots on the forehead. The only exception to this is the use of henna (mehndi).

At the end of your period, you need to take a special bath or ghusl to purify yourself. This is done in a specific way to ensure that the body is completely clean. You cannot begin to pray or fast until you have performed your ghusl correctly.

How to Perform Ghusl

A simple step by step guide:

Before starting your ghusl you should remove any rings, earrings etc. This ensures that absolutely no part of the body is left dry during ghusl, otherwise it is not valid.

When you perform the ghusl you are not just purifying yourself outwardly but also cleansing your inward self, which Insha Allah will lead to a clean heart and soul.

It is liked by Allah to carry out the following before the ghusl:

1. Begin with the name of Allah and make the intention while washing your hands up to the wrist.
2. Remove filth (if any) from the body.
3. Wash your private parts.
4. Perform wudu.

The ghusl consist of three fard (obligatory) acts:

1.   Rinsing the mouth.
2.   Rinsing the nose.
3.   Washing the entire body: wash your entire body three times, starting each time from the head, followed by the right side of the body, then the left, till the toes. You should rub your body the first time you wash it.

You MUST ensure that the above acts are performed otherwise your ghusl is not complete which will mean that any worship you carryout after the ghusl will not be accepted.

When performing your ghusl try your best not to:

1.   Face the direction of the Qiblah.
2.   Waste water as this is sinful and blame worthy.

By the end of your ghusl no part of your body should be left dry.

It is also recommended to cut your finger and toe nails as well as removing the underarm and pubic hair.

How else can we care for our bodies?

As well as taking care of our bodies from the outside we also need to take care of our body from the inside.

You can do this by making sure that you are eating a balanced and healthy diet with not too much junk food.

This helps to maintain a healthy weight and may prevent serious problems such as heart disease and diabetes in later life. You must also take care that everything you eat is halal and that means that you must read the labels on food packets to see that they do not contains anything haram, e.g alcohol, gelatine, pork etc. As well as eating healthily, you also need to ensure that you take regular exercise. In fact, it is a sunnah to exercise and to keep fit and healthy. However, you must remember that it is haram to attend gyms, sports halls and swimming pools at the same time as men.

You may be bombarded with images of thin girls on TV and magazines and made to feel that you should be on a diet so that you too will look thin. But you need to know that thin does not necessarily mean beautiful. If you eat a healthy and balanced diet and get a moderate amount of exercise, then you are beautiful no matter what your shape or size. Remember 'Allah does not look at your outward appearance but only your hearts and deeds.' (Hadith from Sahih Muslim) As long as Allah is happy with us, then why should we care what other people think?

Some of the people in your school may smoke, drink and even take non-prescription drugs. They may think that they are cool. But the only thing that they are doing is destroying their bodies and making themselves ill. Drinking makes you lose control of the situation you are in and that is definitely not cool. Smoking discolours your teeth and can often lead to heart disease and cancer - how can that be a good thing? Just remember that all of these things are strictly haram.

> "Allah loves those who turn to Him constantly and He loves those who keep themselves pure and clean."
> (Surah al-Baqarah 2: 222)

Parting Words

So we have taken a brief journey into what you can expect while you are growing up.

You may be feeling a bit scared about what is happening and you may also be feeling confused about your identity as a Muslimah. The best advice I can give you is to keep remembering Allah through the good and happy times as well as the difficult times.

The most simple but most effective thing you can do at any time is to pray to Allah for direction and remember your purpose and goal in life. Be proud to be a Muslim and stand up for your beliefs. Remember your aim in life is to please Allah not your friends. Islam is about respect, kindness and decency. You should keep clean, dress decently, keep good company and speak good language. This is what makes you beautiful - the kind of person you are and how you treat people - not the way you dress and your accessories.

You should try to learn what is in the Qur'an and the Hadith and follow it with certainty.

I pray Allah showers you with the very best in both worlds. May your every action be governed with the remembrance of the Almighty. May Allah give you the tawfiq (guidance/ability) to flock to good gatherings allowing you to receive, act upon and deliver what you learn to the people around you and beyond- making you true ambassadors of the Deen.

I pray you are amongst those who express shukr (gratitude) in times of joy and sabr (patience) in matters which upset you. May you be of service to all those you meet and fulfill the duties towards your parents in the most pleasing of ways. May you be forever rightly guided and be amongst the best of creation who self-evaluates before judging another.

I pray you keep firm in your ibadah (worship) and hold tight to your Muslim identity. Enjoy these precious years to come and be sure to build a good solid foundation which you will base your life long decisions upon. May your every thought, move and saying mirror the beauty, purity and compassion employed by Allah's Habib ﷺ.

> "Fear Allah wherever you may be; follow up an evil deed with a good one which will wipe (the former) out, and behave good-naturedly towards people."
> (at-Tirmidhi)

Quick Quiz

Circle the answer that applies most to you and then see how you have done on page 54

---

1. Do you perform your salah five times a day?

Always   Mostly   Sometimes   Never

---

2. Do you read the Qur'an every day?

Always   Mostly   Sometimes   Never

3. How often do you cover your hair in front of non-mahrams?

Always   Mostly   Sometimes   Never

4. Are you careful about not buying or wearing tight-fitting clothing, transparent clothes, short sleeves?

Always   Mostly   Sometimes   Never

5. Do you show respect for your elders by not answering back to them or being rude to them?

Always   Mostly   Sometimes   Never

6. Are you careful about not listening to music?

Always   Mostly   Sometimes   Never

7. Are you mindful about how you use the internet?

Always   Mostly   Sometimes   Never

8. How much time do you spend on social networking sites?

Always   Mostly   Sometimes   Never

**Find which answer you have circled the most
number of times and see what it says about you:**

'Always' Well done! You seem to be aware of your Islamic duties and are careful about fulfilling them. Keep it up!

'Mostly' Good for you! You are mostly aware of what you should be doing, you just need to push yourself a bit more.

'Sometimes' You do know right from wrong but you don't always practise it. Do you find yourself behaving differently around different people or in different places? Remember that Allah is everywhere. You have nothing to lose and everything to gain by doing the right thing.

'Never' Well done for being honest. Try to make a small resolution at the beginning of each week or month and then stick to it. It will become easier to incorporate Islamic habits into your daily life.

Suggested Reading

- **A Mother's Rights**
  Matina Wali Muhammad

- **Fatima Az-Zahra**
  Ahmad Thomson

- **Muslim Teenagers Coping**
  Ruqaiyyah Waris Maqsood

- **The Noble Woman**
  Aliya Butt

- **The Sahabiyat**
  Jameelah Jones